40

IRREFUTABLE

—————— *steps to building a* ——————

SUBSTANTIAL

SPEAKING BUSINESS

40

IRREFUTABLE

— *steps to building a* —

SUBSTANTIAL

SPEAKING BUSINESS

STEVE GILLILAND, CSP, CPAE

Chairman & Co-founder, Speaker U™

Advantage®

Published by Advantage, Charleston, South Carolina.
Member of Advantage Media Group.

ADVANTAGE is a registered trademark and the Advantage colophon is a trademark of Advantage Media Group, Inc.

Printed in the United States of America.

ISBN: 978-1-59932-501-9
LCCN: 2014935006

This publication is designed to provide accurate and authoritative information in regard to the subject matter covered. It is sold with the understanding that the publisher is not engaged in rendering legal, accounting, or other professional services. If legal advice or other expert assistance is required, the services of a competent professional person should be sought.

Advantage Media Group is proud to be a part of the Tree Neutral® program. Tree Neutral offsets the number of trees consumed in the production and printing of this book by taking proactive steps such as planting trees in direct proportion to the number of trees used to print books. To learn more about Tree Neutral, please visit **www.treeneutral.com**. To learn more about Advantage's commitment to being a responsible steward of the environment, please visit **www.advantagefamily.com/green**

Advantage Media Group is a publisher of business, self-improvement, and professional development books and online learning. We help entrepreneurs, business leaders, and professionals share their Stories, Passion, and Knowledge to help others Learn & Grow. Do you have a manuscript or book idea that you would like us to consider for publishing? Please visit **advantagefamily.com** or call **1.866.775.1696**.

INTRODUCTION

This book is not about how to make money by consulting, coaching, or hosting webinars. *It provides guidelines for speakers who want to get more bookings to speak.* The book outlines the 40 steps that Steve Gilliland uses to get booked for speaking engagements over 100 times a year. This step-by-step strategy enables Steve to participate in the National Speakers Association (NSA) Million Dollar Speakers Group (MDSG). The book was written to give you confidence and to illustrate that there is a blueprint available with which you can build your own speaking business.

Steve created Speaker U, the first and only online university in which a documented, proven step-by-step program exists for the speaking industry. He is a member of the NSA who has earned his Certified Speaking Professional (CSP) designation, and he is a member of the Council of Peers Award for Excellence (CPAE) Speaker Hall of Fame. Paradoxically, Steve has always flown below the radar, but in the world of meeting planners and speakers bureaus, he is not only noticed, he is at the top of the industry.

While many may lay claim to being the most sought-after speaker, Steve Gilliland's proof lies in his actual numbers. Between 2009 and 2013, he had 584 paid speaking engagements and generated over $7 million in revenue from speaking. He can be heard daily on SiriusXM Satellite Radio's *Laugh USA*, and his books *Enjoy The Ride*, *Making a Difference*, and *Hide Your Goat*, are consistently on the Advantage Media Group bestseller list.

Steve's secret is simple. He has developed processes and procedures for every aspect of his business. His strategic marketing plan is unparalleled in the speaking industry. The student enrollment at Speaker U includes CSPs, recipients of the CPAE, speakers representing five countries, and personnel from management companies who manage speakers.

In the pages ahead, Steve shares his 40 irrefutable steps to building a substantial speaking business.

STEP 1
CREATE A WOW PACKAGE

When a meeting planner is selecting a speaker, you need a *knockout punch to be the one selected.* If everything is equal, what will separate you from the other speakers who are making proposals? You need the meeting planners to say, "Wow!" when they are looking at your information.

These *core items* are the heart and soul of *who* you are and *why* they should hire you. This is the steak!

> » Brand Brochure
>
> » Testimonial Letters Brochure
>
> » One Sheet Biography
>
> » Clients By Industry Brochure
>
> » Products Brochure

These *bells and whistles* are the one-of-a-kind items that distinguish you from the other speakers and make a meeting planner take notice. This is the sizzle!

» Cover Sheet

» Custom Page Dividers

» Personalized Popcorn, with your name and logo on it

» Preview DVD Brochure

» Signed Copy of Your Book

From the minute your package arrives, to the moment it is opened, it should *create an experience that says, "Wow!"* Although we tend to agree that you shouldn't judge a book by its cover, instinctively we all do. Because of this, presentation is everything. Pull out all of the stops and make sure the outside packaging is exceptional and pay the extra money to send it priority, because, after all, getting booked is your priority.

» Binder

» Slip Case

» Priority Mail

STEP 2

CONSTRUCT A MEETING-PLANNER-FRIENDLY WEBSITE

Your competitive edge is *your brilliance.* Your brilliance is one special aspect of yourself that deserves to be elevated into a bright focus across all your marketing efforts. Ask yourself these questions:

> » What are my special talents and unique abilities?

> » What will my clients remember me for?

> » Have I integrated these talents and abilities into my website?

Whoever visits your site has an obvious interest. A *landing page* can quickly tell them how fast you will meet their needs. It should include these items:

» Hire Me! (Video Clip)

» Purchase Product! (Images of your products)

Your site must communicate *why I should hire you*, and do it promptly and succinctly. It should include the following:

» Your Availability (Booking Information / Schedule)

» Your Likeability (Video Preview / Biography)

» Usability (Keynote Speeches / Breakout Sessions)

» Your Credibility (Clients / Letters / Awards / eArticles / Resources)

Your website should *be consistent with all of your marketing strategies* and communicate reliable information to your advocates.

» For Meeting Planners (Link)

» Speaker Bureau (Alternative Site)

Your website isn't created for your ego but to *solve the users' needs*. The priority should be on practicality and usability.

STEP 3

PRODUCE MARKETING MATERIALS TO PROMOTE YOURSELF

A *postcard* is an affordable and effective way to provide a great bang for your marketing bucks. The following are types of postcards and who they should be sent to:

» Brand (Previous Clients)

» Brand (Generic)

» "It's Time" (Previous Clients)

» "This is the Year" (Holds Released)

» One Sheet Supplement

A *one sheet supplement* provides the opportunity to communicate directly with your customer to build a personal relationship. It allows you to reach your target audience with direct messages.

Unlike email, you at least know your *local lead pool* physical mailings will not be routed to a junk folder, never to be seen by the recipient.

Clients warrant some kind of acknowledgement from you, and a well crafted custom *greeting card* and *envelope* can do the job. Receiving a greeting card for any of the following occassions can make someone feel extraordinary.

- » Thank You
- » Referral
- » Anniversary

When the presentation is over, whatever is in the *back of the room* will determine how they will remember you, contact you and recommend you.

It is the little things that go *above and beyond* the norm, differentiate one business from another, and influence customers to make the right choice.

STEP 4

DESIGN A PREVIEW VIDEO THAT GETS YOU NOTICED

The *biggest mistake* speakers make in designing their preview video is that they forget the primary reason a meeting planner looks at the video—the planner wants to see you *speaking!*

Eighty-two percent of Internet users watch more than one billion videos online every day, therefore, remove the guess work and meet the masses where they are.

» Hook them with a professional *introduction* that screams you are successful

» Prove your *credibility* with trustworthiness and expertise

» Your *brilliance* is what they will remember

> » The *closing* is the grand finale to solidify a meeting planner's decision

You set yourself apart from your competition through the *placement and promotion* in your video footage, which makes your customers aware of your products and services.

If the expertise you require to produce this preview product is not available within your company, you should go outside. The right vendor can produce a quality product and may save you money. Some of the services you may need include:

> » Video (Editing / Voiceover / Music)
>
> » Video (Duplication & Thermal Label)
>
> » Packaging and Graphics (DVD Booklet and Thermal Label)
>
> » Printing (DVD Booklet)

STEP 5

BUILD RELATIONSHIPS WITH SPEAKERS BUREAUS

If you want speakers bureaus to have you on their radar, you must *initiate the relationship* and *prove yourself.* To get started, visit:

> » IASB (International Association of Speakers Bureaus) http://www.iasbweb.org

Speakers bureaus receive hundreds of requests for speakers. You need to *build the relationship* and *give them a reason to recommend you!*

> » Give them the booking (Confirmed Event)
>
> » Give them the lead (Letter & Database)
>
> » Give them the reason (preview opportunity)

» Give them the resources (eSpeakers)

To *grow the relationship,* you have to go above and beyond expectations and *support their efforts* without hindering them.

» Holds

» Conference Call (Sell Yourself)

» Frequently Asked Questions (Help Them Sell You)

» Speaker's Showcase (15 minutes)

To *sustain and nurture the relationship,* use soft marketing; let them discover you are genuine and unlike other speakers.

You need to *manage the relationship* by informing speakers bureaus of what they can expect from you, and you need to know what to expect from them.

STEP 6

IDENTIFY THE DIRECT MARKETS TO TARGET

The largest target market I've been able to tap into is the Society for Human Resource Management (SHRM) Annual Conference and Exposition which has hundreds of sessions and is the world's largest human resource marketplace.

Vistage is an organization providing professionally facilitated peer advisory groups that help CEOs, business owners, and senior executives become better leaders, make better decisions, and ultimately achieve better results. Here are some of the events offered by Vistage:

> » All-city Events – These full-day events bring together members, chairs, and their guests from one market.

» Trusted Advisor Partner Forums – These half-day events are held exclusively for trusted advisor members, chairs and their guests.

» National Chief Executive Conference – A Vistage experience like no other, this is the largest national gathering of members and chairs.

Maybe the toughest and most challenging direct market is the U.S. government, however, it is also the largest and most lucrative. The government does not haggle over your published fee. You must fulfill these requirements in order to contract with the government:

» You must be registered with Dun and Bradstreet, which will provide you with a D&B data universal numbering system (DUNS®) number specific to your business.

» Once you receive your DUNS number, go to http://www.sam.gov and create a user account, then register your business. This website and database are part of the System for Award Management (SAM).

» Go to the US General Services Administration website at http://www.gsa.gov for more information. For businesses without GSA contracts, the previous two steps (regarding acquiring the Dun and Bradstreet number) are required. There is an alternative to getting on the

General Services Administration schedule, which is to go to the Federal Business Opportunities website (http://www.fbo.gov) and register to be notified of opportunities in the speaking industry.

Contacting a Convention and Visitors Bureau (CVB) is usually the first step when planning to speak at an organization's getaway or annual meeting. CVBs are designed to offer localized information that is critical for event planning.

STEP 7

FOCUS ON REPEATABLE BUSINESS

The customers you need to grow your company are already doing business with you. A well-defined *previous clients strategy* is required to hit this target.

- » Build an unbeatable bundle of products and services

- » Give clients an incentive to come back

- » Know your trophy clients and recruit them to become advocates

- » Find out what a client wants and give it to him

People who hire speakers for events make decisions every day based on impressions. One of the most important *previous clients tactics* is to put your name in front of them.

» Immediate (Cookies / Quiz Insert / Thank You Card)

» Every 60 Days (Branded Brochure)

» Every Six Months (Branded Postcard)

» Every Year (Anniversary Card)

» Annual (Holiday Card)

» Two Years (It's Time Postcard)

» Constant Contact

» Three Years (Personal Letter)

» New Product

Every time you are on hold to speak at an event you are on a shortlist of potential speakers for the event. If the client releases the hold on your calendar, categorize the potential client as *holds released* and *repeatable business*.

» Send Thank You Card (Personalized)

» Email

» Nine-month Letter (After Original Hold Date)

» Postcard (This is the Year)

» New Product

STEP 8 ○🎤——————————————————

CONSIDER SPECIAL EVENTS

Face-to-face marketing *opportunities* are non-sales-oriented ways of having a personal impact on individuals and groups.

You can generate leads, find new clients, and maintain or improve your current clients' perceptions at trade shows. You can also use a trade show to introduce a new product or launch a new strategy.

> » National Associations (Industry)
>
> » Confirmed Events (Attendees)
>
> » Trade Groups (Meeting Planners)

Consider having a *trade show booth.*

> » Skyline (20-foot Booth)

» Pop Up Banner

▫ Author of the Year

▫ SHRM's # one Rated Speaker

▫ SiriusXM Radio

▫ *Hide Your Goat* (New Book)

There are four *key groups* that are powerful associations for meeting and event professionals. These groups believe in the unequalled power of events and human connections to advance organizational objectives.

» Event Planners Association (EPA)

» Meeting Professionals International (MPI)

» American Society of Association Executives (ASAE)

» American Society for Training and Development (ASTD)

STEP 9

GENERATE INQUIRIES AND CREATE SYSTEMS TO SUPPORT THEM

The most important part of the sales and service process is the step you take to generate an inquiry.

These are the must-dos and must-haves at every event:

» Bookmarks

» Business Cards

» Back-of-the-Room Marketing Materials

» Listen

» Ask Attendees Questions About Speaking Opportunities

> » Collect Business Cards

Be sure your inquiry methods are user friendly and consistent, and allow you to *collect appropriate information* necessary to follow up effectively.

> » Website (To hire Steve Gilliland)
>
> » Telephone (Toll Free)
>
> » On-site (Speaker Lead Form)

When there is an inquiry, the key is to familiarize the potential client with you and your brand. Never assume the person who made the inquiry is the decision maker.

Employ a **multi-touch marketing** approach.

> » Email (Acknowledge Inquiry)
>
> » Phone (Leave Message if Necessary)
>
> » Letter (Wow Package)
>
> » Outbound Call (Discuss Information)
>
> » Obtain a Hold Date

STEP 10 ●━━━━━━━━━━━━━━━━━━━━━━━━━

EMPLOY OTHER SPEAKERS TO BECOME ADVOCATES

The late Zig Ziglar used to say, "If you *help enough people get what they want,* you will eventually get what you want."

The following are four main foundations to *enlist speakers.*

- » NSA Chapter Meeting Follow-up
  - ▫ Personal Note (Business Cards Collected)
  - ▫ Special Note (Monthly Speaker)
  - ▫ Become a Member (Not a Guest)
  - ▫ Volunteer for a Committee
- » National Speakers Association (same methods for NSA Chapter Meeting Follow-up)

- □ Personal Note (Business Cards Collected)
- □ Special Note (Monthly Speaker)
- □ Become a Member (Not a Guest)
- □ Volunteer on a Committee
- » Speakers Bureau Websites
  - □ Equivalent Fee Range
  - □ Research Related Topics
- » Toastmasters

Agree on a *reciprocity plan* with other speakers.

- » Formulate Your List (Key Speakers)
- » Speaker Referral Agreement (10 Percent of Fee)
- » Post Program Referral (Direct)
- » Post Program Referral (Through Bureau)
- » Referral Information (For Speakers)
- » Referral (Build Master List)

STEP 11

SOLICIT CLIENTS TO PROVIDE REFERRALS

Current clients have the capacity to refer you to a prospective client; consequently, do not hesitate to ask them for a referral.

The Overall Strategy:

> » Recruit clients as proactive advocates
>
> » Send them a thank you gift for the referral
>
> » Keep the referral source in the loop

The *referral process* is the formula to getting the referral source to introduce you to the prospective referral client.

» Referral Email – The initial email will focus on reminding the current client how you were either recommended or referred to them; in turn it asks them to do the same.

» Referral Received – Once a client provides a referral, send them a thank you gift.

» Introduction Email with Sample Email – Five days after the thank you gift is mailed, send an email requesting that the client (your referral source) introduce you to the prospective referral client. Attach a sample email for the convenience of the referral source.

» Wow Package and Letter – To support the referral, mail a Wow package and letter to the prospective referral client, and then make a subsequent phone call to verify that they received the information.

You realize *referral success* when the prospective referral client confirms you to speak. Then send a noteworthy gift.

Important Note: In the event a prospective referral doesn't confirm you to speak, add him to your *holds released* or *leads* database for future sales and marketing efforts.

STEP 12

UTILIZE LOCAL LEAD POOL INFORMATION FROM eSPEAKERS

Use the eSpeakers platform and their *local lead pool* service to receive a list of premium leads—people who hire speakers— for each of your engagements. *Turn every event into a sales opportunity* when you leverage hundreds of names, phone numbers, and addresses for potential local buyers.

Every time you confirm an event, eSpeakers provides relevant contacts within about an hour's drive of your engagement. These contacts include:

> » Local Speakers Bureaus

> » Local Chambers of Commerce

> » Association Meeting Planners

» Corporate Meeting Planners

» Previous Clients

» Local Media

Two options to optimize the *local lead pool targeted contacts:*

» Choose whom you want contacted and assign your staff to contact the leads via telephone, email, or physical mailings.

» Employ the eSpeakers sales team to make the calls for you. ($30 USD per hour for *professional* level customers, and $40 USD per hour for *plus* and *starter* level customers.)

Design marketing tools to support your local lead pool contact strategy.

» One-sheets

» Announcement Card (City & Date)

» Email (Established Speakers Bureaus Invitation)

» Email (Potential Client Preview Response)

» Email (Potential Client Preview Details)

» Client Contract (Permission)

STEP 13

MAIL TO PREVIOUS CLIENTS, HOLDS RELEASED AND LEADS

Target Marketing's sixth annual media usage forecast found that direct mail had a rate of 34 percent for new customer acquisition as compared to 25 percent for email marketing.

Give *previous clients* a reason to bring you back. If you are one of the best speakers they have ever had, remind them!

> » Follow Up Mailing # One – Branded Brochure (60 Days)
>
> » Follow Up Mailing # Two – Branded Postcard (Six Months)
>
> » Follow Up Mailing # Three – Anniversary Card (One Year)

» Holiday Card (Annual)

» "It's Time" Postcard (Two years)

» Personal Letter (Three years)

» Announcement – Something New!

You were on a short list prior to a prospect releasing the hold on your calendar. A *holds-released prospect* needs to hear and see a key message along with your name several times.

» Cover Letter and Branded Brochure (Nine months)

» "This is the Year" Postcard (One year)

» Branded Postcard (Two years)

» Personal Letter and Branded Brochure (Three years)

» Announcement – Something New!

Every lead is like a scratch-off lottery ticket. You don't know what you have until you scratch the wax off the face and see what you've won.

» Follow Up (always, all the time, no exceptions)

» "This is the Year" Postcard (One Year)

STEP 14

BRAND YOURSELF BY MAILING TO DIRECT MARKETS

The Three Cs of Branding:

> » Clarity
>
> » Consistency
>
> » Constancy

Focus on mailing and emailing to *SHRM* chapters, state councils and regions.

> » More than 575 affiliated SHRM chapters offer local activities.
>
> » SHRM's state councils provide HR professionals with programs, published materials, conferences,

and more. They also serve as entry points for HR professionals new to a particular state or for those in an area not covered by a local chapter.

» SHRM-affiliated chapters and state councils are divided geographically into five regions. Each of the regions has a council composed of the state council directors in each of the five regions.

Send a mailing to the Senior Client Services Advisor for *Vistage.*

» Vistage International, Inc.
11452, El Camino Real
Suite 400
San Diego, CA 92130

Go to gsa.gov and be prepared to do some heavy lifting to penetrate the *government speaking market.*

Select 100 *convention and visitors bureaus* and mail your brand brochure.

» http://www.cvent.com/rfp/us-cvb-directory-84666a30191e407ea182af64c488696a.aspx

STEP 15

BRAND YOURSELF BY MAILING TO EXCLUSIVE INDUSTRIES

Select up to four different industries and create specific **supplemental** *one-sheets* that will appeal to a particular industry meeting planner.

Examples:

> » Banking
>
> » Automobile Dealers
>
> » Health Care
>
> » Education

Supplemental one-sheets should include the following information:

- » Your particular clients within the industry

- » A testimonial letter specific to the industry

- » A powerful quote from someone within the industry

- » Terminology exclusive to the industry

- » The takeaways attendees will receive from your presentation

- » A statement from you validating your knowledge of the industry

Two core reasons why *supplemental mailings* work:

- » 73 percent of consumers prefer direct mail over email; 18 percent prefer e-mail

- » 79 percent of people read or skim their junk mail

STEP 16

BRAND YOURSELF BY MAILING TO ASSOCIATIONS

A trade association—also known as an industry trade group, business association, or sector association—is an organization founded and funded by businesses that operate in a specific industry.

Prepare and send a mailing to the **top 10 associations** in the world.

> » AARP (formerly the American Association of Retired Persons)
>
> » American Chemical Society
>
> » National Education Association (NEA)
>
> » National Rifle Association (NRA)

- » American Diabetes Association

- » American Petroleum Institute

- » American Psychological Association (APA)

- » Society for Human Resource Management (SHRM)

- » Association of American Medical Colleges (AAMC)

- » American Association for the Advancement of Science (AAAS)

Another resource is The Planning Shop, an organization that provides resources for entrepreneurs and small business. Go to their website at http://www.planningshop.com/associations, and target specific associations who would be intrigued by your message.

STEP 17

PURCHASE INDUSTRY-SPECIFIC SOFTWARE

Look as competent and polished behind the scenes as you do standing in front of an audience.

Exclusive software from **eSpeakers** can administer every aspect of your speaking business. Here are some of the topics covered:

  » When & Where

  » Contacts

  » Travel

  » Action List

  » Services

» Customizing Your Business

» Library

You need the capability to design reports that will help you analyze your business.

» Current Events (Event Details)

» Schedule & Events (Events List) for current year
  □ Include holds
  □ Include only events with offer pending

» Business Intelligence
  □ Income (Include confirmed events)
  □ Productivity By Bureau

There are numerous advantages to using eSpeakers, including the capacity to create your own "bureau friendly" link. You can then forward the link to potential bureau clients that need all of the information in one place. You can also use this same feature for prospective direct clients.

STEP 18

DESIGN A DETAILED PLAN TO MANAGE HOLDS

The goal is to *turn every hold into a confirmed event.*

First and foremost, determine your *speaking fee.*

> » Don't overprice yourself
>
> » Be able to explain why you charge what you do
>
> » Your fee should always be based on the great value you provide

Set a *hold policy* to avoid confusion among clients and staff.

> » Full fee
>
> » Negotiated fee

>> Hold sequence

Employ methods that promote you and nudge prospective clients.

>> Hold Letter

>> Hold Email (Administration)

 □ Industry-specific Clients

 □ Industry-specific Testimonial Letters

>> Hold Email (Speaker)

 □ Thank You

 □ Accessibility

Design an *offer pending* policy to ensure that you and the clients are both protected.

>> Date verification

>> Required steps

>> Required information

STEP 19

DESIGN A DETAILED PLAN FOR CONFIRMED EVENTS

A deal is not sealed until the contract is signed. Reinforce the client's feeling that they are making the right decision by entering into a contract with you.

- » Set clear deadlines
- » Document all requests for changes
- » Be professional
- » Make sure the program agreement is error free
- » Offer two versions to distinguish expense reimbursement (all-travel /all-inclusive)
- » Have two copies of the program agreement

» Review the program agreement with the client

Knowledge is power. Be sure to design a *program details* form to include:

» Contact Information

» Venue

» Hotel

» Ground Transportation

Once the contract is received, follow a *predetermined set of procedures* to make sure all parts of the process are completed.

» Review and sign the contract

» Scan the program agreement and upload it to the eSpeakers Library

» Scan the program details and upload it to the eSpeakers Library

» Using the eSpeakers program, check the Offer Pending box

» Go to the Action Tab list and confirm

» File information in your client file (more on filing tips in the chapter ahead)

» Email client

Design an *event review process* for all speakers bureau and direct confirmed events.

SPEAKER

STEP 20

ORGANIZE FILES TO PROVIDE ADDED OPPORTUNITIES

Your *filing system* has a huge impact on your success. An excellent filing system enables you to find what you need when you need it. Here are some categories to use:

>> Offer Pending

>> Confirmed Events

>> Clients

Your **client files** are the heart and soul of your business. Previous client files serve a continuous purpose by being connected to your long-term marketing plan.

>> Post-program Follow-up

- » Program Agreement

- » Speaker Agreement

- » Program Details

- » Event Details

- » Conference Call

- » Special Requests (such as Recording Authorization)

- » Speaking-fee Invoice

- » Expense Invoice (Receipts)

- » W-9

- » Proposal (if Applicable)

The eSpeakers software was designed for professional speakers and includes two major *filing gateways* that save you time and money:

- » Library Tab

- » Action List Tab

SPEAKER

STEP 21

DEVELOP A PRE-PROGRAM CHECKLIST FOR YOUR EVENT

Your pre-program checklist should include several items:

- » Weather Report from eSpeakers
- » Pre-purchase Order Form
- » UPS Delivery Confirmation
- » Event Details & Notes from Client
- » Pre-Addressed Thank You Card
- » Label & Gift

To guarantee your event is a success, prepare hard so you can finish easy. When you check in at the hotel, take care of these items:

» Look Who Just Checked In (Postcard)

» Telephone Call

» Locate Program Boxes (Deliver to Room)

» Charge iPad/digital devices

» Press Clothes

» Order Room Service

» Go to Bed Early!

Arrive 90 minutes prior to session start time, not your speaking start time.

» Check in with AV personnel

» Set up Back-of-the-Room

» Pre-sign Books

» Meet with person introducing you

» Begin to mingle with attendees

STEP 22

CONSTRUCT A RETAIL ZONE IN THE BACK-OF-THE-ROOM

You can have a best-selling book or an incredible audio product, but if it is displayed in the wrong location you are not going to sell it.

» Acquire authorization in your contract and/or conference call to sell at the back-of-the-room

» Request two, six-foot tables (skirted)

» Determine the best possible location for table placement

The purpose of *Point of Purchase (POP)* displays is to make a speaker's products appear professional and appealing to the customer's eye. POPs are an integral component of successful marketing. Several POP items may include:

» Payment Tent Card

» Price Tent Card

» Promotional Tent Card

Each product should have an individual price tent card. The cards can be categorized by:

» Specials

» Books

» Audio Books

» CDs

» DVDs

A core component of your overall marketing strategy is the *display of your marketing materials.*

» Branded Brochure

» Business Card

» Product Brochure

» Promotional Card

» eArticle/Email Sign Up Sheet

STEP 23

DEVELOP AN ONSITE POST-PROGRAM STRATEGY

Approach *working the tables in the back-of-the-room* in the same manner you would if you were managing a retail store. Don't be afraid to ask for assistance.

- » Pre-arrange with meeting planner
- » Recruit people to man your table by giving them a complimentary signed copy of your book
- » Accept Cash & Checks
- » Accept Credit Card Payment (Square)

As people begin to gather at the tables, don't be afraid to **let them know what is on the table**. Don't leave the shopping solely to the customer; point out products to encourage increased sales.

» Explain products

» Introduce marketing materials

» See if someone is interested in hiring you to speak at their event

» Let them know the books are already pre-signed

Display the remaining marketing materials on the tables, so that after you leave, people still have the opportunity to take something with them.

Take time to pack up the remaining products properly to avoid damaging books, CDs, or DVDs.

STEP 24

DEVELOP AN OFF-SITE POST-PROGRAM PROCESS

We all know that *good follow-up is vital.* According to the technology research and advisory company Gartner, almost 70 percent of leads are mishandled in some way. So great follow-up will give effective speakers a huge advantage over less rigorous competitors.

The post-program follow-up should include a checklist of items to execute following the completion of a program.

> » Ask for a referral
>
> » Add the client to your database
>
> » Add the client to your website
>
> » Request a testimonial letter

» Execute as many as three follow-up mailings over the next 12 months

» Ship product orders not fulfilled during the program

» Ship remaining product back to your office

» Blog about the program

» Utilize pictures from the event on your website and in your future marketing materials

It is essential to *implement a solid referral process* that persuades and rewards direct clients and speakers for recommending you to their colleagues.

It is equally important to *recommend a speaker to the client* for their next event and then notify the speaker you are endorsing.

STEP 25

CREATE GREAT AUDIO PRODUCTS

From the moment a customer or meeting planner begins listening to your audio, it must make them recognize your value.

The *music and voiceover* are key elements that set the tone for the receptivity of the listener.

A high percentage of people will discard the jewel case, which makes the *thermal label* particularly important when designing audio products.

» Background (match your book color if applicable)

» Presentation Title (same as your book if applicable)

» Speaker Logo

» Producer Logo

» Copyright Disclaimer

The *cover booklet* is your opportunity to design a miniature four-page brochure to sell more products and market yourself.

The *tray liner* is in the back of the CD; this is the "headline" that people read to gauge their interest in purchasing the product. It should feature:

» Speaker Picture

» Condensed Biography (interesting and unique)

» Description (makes them want more)

» Include Track Titles when applicable.

» UPC Code

» Copyright Disclaimer

» Contact Information

Make your audio products available for retail purchase beyond the back-of-the-room sales.

STEP 26

WRITE A BOOK AND FIND A GREAT SELF-PUBLISHER

Unless you are a legitimate *New York Times* or *USA Today* best-selling author, don't let the tail wag the dog. Here are some things to consider when shopping for a publisher:

- » New York Publishing vs. Self-Publishing
- » Ego vs. Common Sense
- » Perceived Marketing vs. Real Marketing
- » Pre-purchase Order Drop Shipments

Your ability to *regulate the process* will keep three key aspects of your book within your control.

- » Credibility

> » Marketability

> » Profitability

The technology age ushered in a generation of people who are "too busy" to read, hence more and more people are listening to *audio books* than ever before.

> » Narration – As the professional speaker who wrote the book, you should be the person reading it for the recording.

> » Unabridged Content – Record it from cover to cover, leaving nothing out.

> » Edit

> » Music

> » Voiceover

SPEAKER U.

STEP 27

MAKE YOUR SIGNATURE PRESENTATION AVAILABLE ON DVD

For every one organization that can afford to pay your speaking fee and would like to hire you, there are five organizations that would like to hire you and cannot afford to pay your speaking fee.

Create a DVD product that is an excellent representation of you and your message.

> » At large events, the client will film the presentation. Be sure to enter into a contractual agreement to acquire the master footage.

> » Set the price point of your DVD to deliver more transactions instead of more dollars per transaction.

» Be sure the venue has at least 500 people and pre-announce the filming for better impact.

The *content* of the DVD should include the following items:

» Graphics to illustrate title

» Music to set the tone

» Menu options to add value

» Introduction to enliven the presentation

» Information on how to schedule you as a speaker

» Invitation to visit your online store

They will judge the DVD by the cover, so design the *front cover* to rock!

» Record your presentation *live* (on location)

» Presentation Title

» Speaker's Name

» Corner ID (DVD - the corner ID will help identify the product best)

Be sure to incorporate an *insert inside the cover*, and make the customer an offer on your other products that they cannot refuse.

STEP 28

BE CAUTIOUS WHEN FASHIONING GIFTS FOR YOUR BRAND

Developing and launching a new product requires a skill level beyond the notion of putting your logo or name on a *gift item*. It includes:

- » Product Development
- » Licensing
- » Marketing
- » Prototyping
- » Manufacturing/Sourcing

There is a big difference between a *retail* gift item and a *promotional* item.

Before you invest your money in gifts around your brand, ask yourself these questions:

» Would you purchase the gift for yourself?

» Would a gift company license your product or carry it in their catalog?

» How does your product compare to similar products in the marketplace?

» Is your gift unique or just another coffee mug with your name and/or logo on it?

» Is your gift related to your brand and will it enhance you as a speaker and your other products?

STEP 29

CREATE AN INDEPENDENT ONLINE STORE

Don't clutter *product pages* with dense text and frivolous functionality. Instead, follow these steps:

» Make the "Add to Cart" and "Proceed to Checkout" buttons clear, consistent, and highly visible.

» Product pages need to load fast and be easy to respond to.

» Use high-resolution photos and images. Product photos, particularly for books and CDs, are critical for building confidence and giving the user a strong grasp of what it is they're actually buying.

» Keep copy concise and highlight the key points. Use bullets to help visitors read and digest these points quickly.

» Provide product reviews and testimonials from other customers who have purchased the product, and position useful reviews at the top of the product listing.

Utilize *links* that are clear-cut, to the point, and easy to navigate. For example, links to categories should be as easy as:

» Books

» Audio Books

» CDs

» DVD Set

» Specials

» Group Discounts

» Return Policy

» Frequently Asked Questions (FAQs)

» Printable Order Form

Give customers the opportunity to preview all of your products.

» Select the best three or four pages out of your book and make it available for your customers to read.

» Select the best story from your CD and make it available for them to hear.

» Produce a live clip that will begin playing when customers arrive at your DVD page. Don't even make them have to click!

STEP 30

DEVELOP A PRESELL STRATEGY FOR YOUR PRODUCTS

Once you are confirmed to speak at an event, shift your focus to **preselling your books and CDs** to the meeting planner. Items to help support the meeting planner's buy-in are:

- » Pre-purchase Letter
- » Volume Discount One Sheet
- » Conference Call Sheet

You never know where a prospect is in the sales process unless you stay in contact long enough to find out. With each *contact follow-up* you make, you increase the odds that a client will act on your offer. Sample follow-up methods may include:

- » Sending a physical mailing

> » Following-up with a phone call

> » Scheduling a conference call

On the conference call you can ask them, "Are you giving the attendees anything to take home from the conference?" You can also make the suggestion, "Something you may want to consider is giving everyone a signed copy of my book to reinforce what they will hear."

Strategic business partnerships give you the opportunity to grow and improve your business by having a partner strengthen and complement your business. Here are some areas where a partner can help:

> » Warehouse the product

> » Process the pre-purchase order

> » Drop-ship the order

STEP 31

SELL YOUR PRODUCTS SUBLIMINALLY WHILE SPEAKING

Subliminal messaging has been shown to be effective in leading the way for individual responses and stimulating emotional activity in the subconscious. In order to capitalize on this, be sure to incorporate the following when speaking:

» Mention your products in your speaker introduction

» Place a bookmark featuring your book at every seat

» Tell a signature story from the book

» Tell a funny story about something that happened to you at a book signing

As I was sitting signing books prior to an event a woman approached me and said, "Did you write that?" I said, "No. I just saw a pile of books sitting here on this table and thought I would sit down and sign my name in them."

When appropriate, *reference something from your book* that draws attention to your book.

> » Quote
>
> » Story
>
> » Poem
>
> » If the room is arranged banquet style, with round tables without a centerpiece, make your book the centerpiece—if its title is the same as your presentation. (You can actually suggest to the client that he give the book away to a person who has a marker of some kind taped under his seat. Give the lucky winner a good discount on additional products).

STEP 32

CREATE A PROCESS TO GENERATE ADDITIONAL SALES

Only **two percent** of sales are produced on the first contact.

- » Three percent of sales are made on the second contact
- » Five percent of sales are made on the third contact
- » 10 percent of sales are made on the fourth contact

Be consistent in following up with customers who purchased products from you.

- » Thank You Letter (for pre-purchased books)
- » Thank You Card (purchased at the program)

» Constant Contact Promotion (email blast promotion to your list)

» Customer Database

Create a *customer database* of people who have purchased products from you.

The next time you *prerelease* a book, CD, or DVD, contact all of your previous customers who have already bought something from you.

People are curious, so give them a reason to not only visit your back-of-the-room display, but also to *take something* with them. Items to help encourage the sale on site include:

» Order Form

» Product Brochure

» Bags

» Bag Advertisement Insert

» Prerelease Sign-up Sheet

STEP 33

PREPARE TIRELESSLY BEFORE WALKING ON STAGE

Know your stuff. Never stop reading, listening, and learning.

Learn everything you can about *your client's products, services and culture.* This will help you relate and resonate best with your audience.

>> Visit their website

>> Ask questions on the conference call

>> Learn and speak with key personnel

You have to *attract others' attention* by connecting early in your presentation. Relate to your audience by tapping into a personal place for them, perhaps a family member, significant event in their life, etc.

- » Mother and Father
- » Children
- » Spouse

People must be interested in your words and believe in what you're saying.

- » Be relevant
- » Be genuine
- » Be humble
- » Be polite
- » Be friendly
- » Make them smile early
- » Make sure that your pace is right for the audience — not too fast or slow
- » Speak from your heart, not your head

STEP 34

BE PROFESSIONAL BACK STAGE AND ON STAGE

You are a "guest speaker" at the event, which means **you are a guest**. Unless you are a celebrity, people did not attend the event to see you and only you. For this reason, pay close attention to the following:

» Don't require special drinks, lighting, music or anything else that can be perceived as you being "high maintenance."

» Regardless of when you start, finish on time.

» Use whatever microphone resonates the best in the room. Sometimes what you desire isn't the best acoustical fit for the venue. Ask the AV team for their opinion.

» Don't try new material at "signature" events.

» Be careful not to tell too many jokes. Tell funny stories. When they are laughing they are listening. When they are listening they are learning.

» Never cross the line with questionable material and language that would not be accepted by 100 percent of the audience.

STEP 35

BE REAL ON STAGE

When you have finished speaking, you will not only be judged by the message you delivered, but whether they **believed you** can live by the message you delivered. In order to make sure you stay true to yourself, on stage and off, follow these rules of thumb:

» Learn from others, but be yourself.

» Learn from your own mistakes.

» Be humble and share your mistakes.

» Never apologize for who you are, where you have been, or what you have done.

» Be who you are off stage.

» Remind yourself of the responsibility you have on stage.

» Never be afraid to share your faith.

STEP 36

BE REMEMBERED ON STAGE

The greatest compliment you will ever receive is when someone asks you to **repeat something** you said. This not only means they were listening, but what you said stuck with them, it resonated and sparked something in them that made them not want to forget what you shared. To maintain this type of relationship with your audiences, it is important to incorporate the following into your presentation:

» Be quotable

» Be distinctive

» Be spontaneous

» Start with a story that grabs their attention

» End with a story they will never forget

» End where you started; by coming full circle, you reiterate your message through and through

STEP 37

RUN YOUR COMPANY AS A CORPORATE ENTITY

Your corporate structure will depend on the **financial path** you are ultimately planning on going down.

There are three main **reasons** to become incorporated:

> » Protect personal assets
>
> » Save on taxes
>
> » Own your own name

There are three corporate **options** when becoming incorporated:

> » S-Corp
>
> » C-Corp

> » LLC

There are pros and cons to each corporate structure; however, an **S-Corp** is most common for professional speakers for the following reasons:

> » Tax benefits when it comes to excess profits known as distributions
>
> » Pays the employees a "reasonable salary," which means it should be tied to industry norms, while also deducting payroll expenses like federal taxes and FICA
>
> » Remaining profits can be distributed to the owners as dividends, which are taxed at a lower rate than income

As a professional speaker it is in your best interest to find a good **Intellectual Property Attorney** in addition to your corporate attorney.

STEP 38

USE QUICKBOOKS PRO FOR YOUR BUSINESS FINANCES

By using a system such as QuickBooks, you are able to clearly create invoices, record revenue, track expenses, and most importantly, get reliable records for tax time.

Create a Chart of Accounts for **travel** as a speaker.

- » Airfare
- » Ground Transportation
- » Hotel
- » Internet & fax
- » Meals
- » Parking

» Tolls

Create a Chart of Accounts exclusively for a **speaking** business.

» Accounting Services

» Advertising

» Bureau Commissions

» Contributions & Donations

» Credit Card Finance Charges

» Graphic Design

» Insurance

» Internet

» Legal Fees

» Marketing Materials

» Membership Fees

» Office Equipment

» Postage

» Printing Costs

» Shipping

» Trade Show

» Website

STEP 39

AS YOUR BUSINESS GROWS, HIRE THE RIGHT PEOPLE

If you are serious about growing your speaking business, your first employee should be a **sales person**.

The right individual can **build relationships** with many targets and implement your strategic marketing plan to get you booked with any/all of the following:

- » Speakers Bureaus
- » Direct Markets
- » Residual Clients
- » Special Events

After hiring the right person be sure to compensate and incentivize them to perform at a high level. You will get exactly what you pay for! Great incentive offers include:

- » Paid Time Off
- » Vacation Policy
- » Christmas Bonus Plan
- » Profit Bonus Plan
- » Health Insurance
- » Retirement (Simple IRA)

Regardless of the number of employees, create a set of performance metrics and hold people accountable for the following:

- » Attitude
- » Interpersonal Relationships
- » Knowledge of Job
- » Quality of Work
- » Work Habits
- » Initiative
- » Attendance / Dependability

STEP 40

DISCOVER AND FOLLOW A SET OF BEST PRACTICES

Since I began my speaking career in 1999, I have aimed to be regarded as one of the best speakers in the world. I made a conscious choice to not just craft a speech, but create a presentation that would leave a permanent imprint on the hearts of people. I want my presentation to be extremely entertaining and funny, but impossible to replicate because of the emotional content that would resonate and emotionally connect with members of my audiences.

I didn't just practice a little. I practiced a *lot*. I studied speakers, comedians, poets, and actors. At one NSA convention, a speaker said to me that he would give anything to be where I was, to which I replied, "I have."

Over the span of 15 years, I have been asked numerous questions regarding my career, the business I built, and for advice on how to make it to the top in the speaking world. A special feature in my online university, Speaker U, is all of the downloadable files provided in each lesson. The final download available in Speaker U is a list of my Most-Frequently Asked Questions regarding my career. As you graduate from the Speaker U program, you'll be encouraged to take some time to think about how you would answer these questions, and how you might answer them after you have implemented what you learned through Speaker U.

TO APPLY visit SpeakerU.com/Apply or call 866.445.5452 today!

PRAISE FOR SPEAKER U™

"The content is brilliant and the delivery is exceptional. With so many speakers in NSA trying to make money on other speakers, I was skeptical. After the first three courses I realized this was different."

–JAY HEWITT
GREENVILLE, SOUTH CAROLINA

"Well done. Very impressed. Totally worth the investment!"

–DAVE DAVLIN
SAN ANTONIO, TEXAS

"We have never invited back the same speaker to present at our NSA Chapter meetings the next year. After Steve Gilliland presented at our chapter meeting in 2013, we invited him back in 2014. Without question, the information he presented as a highlight to his online university was over-the-top."

–DR. TINA THOMAS
NSA NEW ORLEANS PRESIDENT 2013-14

"When Steve Gilliland was willing to show me his tax returns for the last ten years, I was blown away. He is successful and genuine! Not only was I a student of his online university (Speaker U), but I also reached out to Steve several times and he always returned my calls and responded to my emails."

–LISA RYAN
CLEVELAND, OHIO

"After being a student of Speaker U and experiencing everything you receive, I can honestly say it may be underpriced. How many speakers are willing to give you every process, procedure and marketing strategy down to the letters and emails they have used to be successful? Thanks for sharing everything!"

–SCOTT BURROWS
TAMPA, FLORIDA

CPSIA information can be obtained
at www.ICGtesting.com
Printed in the USA
LVOW05s0922050117
519815LV00032B/411/P